10-Minute Bible Stories for Teens

Olivia Ark

Copyright © 2025 by Olivia Ark

All rights reserved.

No portion of this book may be reproduced in any form without written permission from the publisher or author, except as permitted by U.S. copyright law.

CONTENTS

1. The Creation (Genesis 1) — 1
2. Adam and Eve (Genesis 3) — 5
3. Cain and Abel (Genesis 4) — 8
4. Noah and the Ark (Genesis 6–9) — 11
5. The Tower of Babel (Genesis 11:1–9) — 15
6. The Call of Abraham (Genesis 12:1–9) — 18
7. God's Covenant with Abraham (Genesis 15 & 17) — 21
8. Hagar and Ishmael (Genesis 16; 21:1–21) — 24
9. Sodom and Gomorrah (Genesis 18–19) — 27
10. The Birth of Isaac (Genesis 21:1–7) — 30
11. The Testing of Abraham (Genesis 22:1–19) — 32
12. Jacob's Dream (Genesis 28:10–22) — 35
13. Joseph Sold into Slavery (Genesis 37) — 38
14. Joseph in Egypt (Genesis 39–41) — 41
15. Joseph Reunites with His Family (Genesis 42–50) — 45
16. Moses and the Burning Bush (Exodus 3–4) — 48

17.	The Plagues and the Passover (Exodus 7–12)	51
18.	Crossing the Red Sea (Exodus 14)	55
19.	God Provides Manna (Exodus 16)	58
20.	The Ten Commandments (Exodus 19–20)	61
21.	The Widow's Oil Miracle (2 Kings 4:1-7)	64
22.	Samson's Strength (Judges 13–16)	66
23.	Ruth and Boaz (Ruth)	69
24.	Samuel Hears God's Voice (1 Samuel 3)	72
25.	David and Goliath (1 Samuel 17)	74
26.	David's Heart for God (2 Samuel 6)	78
27.	Solomon's Wisdom (1 Kings 3)	81
28.	Elijah vs. Prophets of Baal (1 Kings 18)	84
29.	Hezekiah's Prayer for Healing (2 Kings 20; Isaiah 38)	87
30.	Esther Saves Her People (Book of Esther)	89
31.	Job's Trials (Book of Job)	92
32.	Jonah and the Big Fish (Book of Jonah)	94
33.	Death & Resurrection of Jesus	97
34.	Daniel in the Lions' Den (Daniel 6)	100
35.	Birth of Jesus (Matthew 1–2; Luke 2)	103
36.	Feeding the 5,000 (Mark 6; John 6)	106
37.	Sermon on the Mount (Matthew 5–7)	109
38.	Jesus' Baptism & Temptation (Matthew 3–4)	112
39.	The Prodigal Son (Luke 15:11–32)	115
40.	The Holy Spirit at Pentecost (Acts 2)	118

41. New Heaven and New Earth (Revelation 21–22)　　　　121

Chapter One

The Creation (Genesis 1)

In the beginning, before time had a name or shape, God hovered over an endless ocean of darkness. With a voice more powerful than any sound known to man, He spoke a single phrase: **"Let there be light."** At once, light burst into existence, chasing away the shadows and drawing the line between day and night.

On the second day, God shaped the skies above—an expanse of brilliant blue stretching across the horizon. Below, He gathered the waters into seas, exposing wide stretches of land on the third day. It was here that life began to bloom. Trees stretched their limbs heavenward, flowers unfurled in a rainbow of colors, and lush grasses swayed in gentle breezes.

Then, God decorated the sky with the sun to rule the day, and the moon and stars to adorn the night, creating a dazzling display that has guided travelers and dreamers ever since. In the seas, God summoned forth fish of every shape and size—some sleek and swift, others flashing vibrant colors. Above the land, birds took flight, their wings catching the wind as they filled the air with song.

On the sixth day, God populated the earth with animals both wild and tame—roaring lions, bounding deer, and playful puppies among them. But the crowning moment came when God bent down to shape a figure out of the dust. Ever so gently, He breathed His own breath into this creation, and Adam opened his eyes to see the world for the first time. Soon, God created Eve so Adam would have a companion—someone with whom to explore this vast, new home.

Together, Adam and Eve walked in the cool of the day, discovering waterfalls, naming animals, and marveling at the warmth of the sun and the softness of the grass beneath their feet. They encountered God Himself in the garden, talking and learning from Him as a child might with a loving parent.

At the end of all this creative work, God stepped back like an artist admiring a masterpiece. He declared it all **"very good."** On the seventh day, He rested, not because He was tired, but to set a pattern for His creation—a holy pause that invites us to celebrate and appreciate the wonders He has made.

Reflection for Today

1. In a busy world, how can you pause to recognize the wonder of God's creation around you?

2. What does the idea that God "breathed" life into humanity tell you about your own value and purpose?

Prayer

Dear Heavenly Father, thank You for shaping this incredible world and for giving us life. Help me to pause in awe of Your masterpiece and to remember that I am wonderfully made. Amen.

Chapter Two

Adam and Eve (Genesis 3)

Adam and Eve lived in a beautiful garden called Eden, a place where every tree bore delicious fruit and each creature roamed peacefully. The grass beneath their feet was soft and inviting, and a gentle breeze often carried the scent of blooming flowers. In the cool of the day, they would walk with God, learning from Him and enjoying the perfect world He had made.

However, in the midst of this paradise stood a single tree that God had told them not to eat from—the Tree of the Knowledge of Good and Evil. Its fruit was bright and enticing, but God's command had been clear: it was off-limits. Adam and Eve accepted this boundary without question at first, trusting that God's wisdom exceeded their own.

Then, one day, a serpent appeared. With cunning eyes and a smooth, persuasive tongue, it slithered beside Eve and whispered, **"Did God really say you must not eat from any tree in the garden?"** The question sowed a tiny seed of doubt in Eve's mind. She knew they could eat from every tree except that one, but the serpent continued, **"You won't really die. God knows that when you eat from it, your eyes will be opened, and you will be like Him, knowing good and evil."**

Drawn by curiosity and the desire to know more, Eve reached out and picked one of the forbidden fruits. Its color was deep and vibrant, and it seemed to glow in her hand. She took a bite, the flavor both sweet and strange. Adam, who was with her, also tasted the fruit she offered.

At that very moment, a cold weight settled in their hearts. Their eyes were opened, but not to the glorious knowledge they expected. Instead, they felt an uncomfortable awareness of their vulnerability—and a sudden urge to hide. Shame, like a heavy cloak, fell over them for the first time. No longer did they feel free to stand openly before God.

When God came for their usual evening walk, Adam and Eve shrank among the trees, desperate to remain unseen. Yet God, who already knew what had happened, called out, **"Where are you?"** Trembling, they emerged and confessed their disobedience. Though grief filled His voice, God still cared for them, crafting clothing to cover their shame. Then, with a heartbroken sigh, He sent them out of Eden, the paradise they had once taken for granted.

Their perfect world had changed. Thorns and hardship awaited them now. Yet God did not abandon Adam and Eve. He left them with a hope that one day, the damage done in the garden would be undone. Even in the midst of their failure, God's love shone through, offering them a path to redemption despite the consequences of their choice.

Reflection for Today

1. Have you ever made a choice that promised excitement but ended up leaving you with guilt or regret?

2. How do you think God's love and forgiveness can help you move forward after a mistake?

Prayer

Merciful God, thank You for loving me even when I fail. Teach me to trust Your wisdom and forgive me when I choose my own path instead of Yours. Amen.

Chapter Three

CAIN AND ABEL (GENESIS 4)

Adam and Eve began their new life outside the Garden of Eden. Though the world felt more rugged and harsh than the paradise they once knew, they held on to the promise that God still loved them. In time, Eve gave birth to two sons: Cain, the firstborn, and then Abel.

As the boys grew, they each found their calling. Cain worked the soil, coaxing crops from the earth and gathering its harvest. Abel raised animals—sheep, goats, and other livestock. The two young men soon learned that everything they had, every blessing, was a gift from God. So when the time came to offer a sacrifice, each brought something from his livelihood: Cain gathered from the fruits of his fields, and Abel brought the firstborn of his flocks, the very best he had to give.

When God received their offerings, He regarded Abel's with favor. Abel's gift came from a heart full of gratitude, offering God the first and finest of his flock. Cain, however, had chosen what was convenient rather than what was truly precious. Although the difference might have seemed minor, God could see Cain's heart—and it was not fully in tune with worship.

Cain grew resentful. Bitterness gnawed at him, and he grew restless under the weight of jealousy. One day, he invited Abel into the fields. There, anger got the better of Cain, and in a tragic burst of rage, he attacked and killed his brother.

Soon, God's voice came, asking, **"Where is your brother Abel?"** Trying to hide his guilt, Cain answered, **"I don't know. Am I my brother's keeper?"** But nothing could be hidden from God. Though His heart ached for both sons—one dead, and the other lost to sin—God confronted Cain's wrongdoing. As punishment, the ground Cain had once tilled so easily would now resist his work. A restless wanderer he would become.

Still, even in His justice, God showed mercy. To protect Cain from revenge, He marked him so that no one would harm him. Cain left his home that day, burdened by regret and the knowledge that his actions had forever changed his family's story. Yet, though he carried the consequences of his choice, God's compassionate concern did not abandon him entirely.

Reflection for Today

1. Have you ever felt jealous of someone else's success or blessings? How might you handle those feelings in a way that honors God?

2. What do you think it means to be your "brother's (or sister's) keeper" in the world today?

Prayer

Heavenly Father, help me to recognize when anger, jealousy, or bitterness stirs in my heart. Teach me to respond with love and humility. Thank You for Your mercy, even when I fail. Amen.

Chapter Four
Noah and the Ark (Genesis 6–9)

As time passed and generations were born, the world grew crowded with people. But it also grew dark with evil. Though God had once looked on His creation with delight, He now saw that nearly everyone's thoughts and actions had turned toward violence and selfishness. Heartbroken, He decided to bring a great flood to wash the earth clean of its corruption.

Yet, in the midst of all this darkness, there was one man who still listened for God's voice: Noah. Though he was far from perfect, Noah was faithful to God. One day, God spoke to him and revealed the plan to send a massive flood. He commanded Noah to build a huge boat—a wooden ark large enough to house his family and animals of every kind. This project must have seemed bizarre to the people around him, especially in a land without oceans nearby. Even so, Noah obeyed.

Day after day, he sawed planks and hammered nails, trusting God's instructions despite the whispers, jeers, and doubts of onlookers.

When the ark was finally finished, God led pairs of animals—lions and lambs, birds and lizards, elephants and insects—into its shelter. Noah and his family boarded, and soon, the clouds gathered overhead. Raindrops began to fall, then thunder roared as the heavens opened. Waters rose higher and higher, lifting the ark until nothing but swirling currents remained.

For forty days and nights, the rain pounded, and the earth lay submerged. Inside the ark, cramped together with the wildlife, Noah's family waited. They had no control over the weather, no steering wheel to guide their ship—only faith that God would keep His promise. Eventually, the rain stopped, and slowly, the waters began to subside.

After many weeks, the ark came to rest on the mountains of Ararat. Noah sent out birds—a raven, then a dove—to search for any sign of dry land. Finally, the dove returned with a small olive leaf in its beak, proof that the floodwaters were receding. Not long after, the ground dried enough for Noah, his family, and all the creatures to step out into a world made fresh and new.

In gratitude, Noah built an altar to worship God. Moved by this act of devotion, God placed a rainbow in the sky—a shimmering promise that He would never again destroy the world with a flood. This vivid arc of color stood as a sign of hope and a reminder that, even in judgment, God extends mercy.

Reflection for Today

1. Have you ever felt alone or misunderstood when trying to do what you believe is right?

2. How can you trust God's promises in situations that seem beyond your control?

Prayer

Faithful God, thank You for keeping Your promises even when everything seems uncertain. Help me to walk in obedience to You, trusting in Your care and provision. Amen.

Chapter Five

The Tower of Babel (Genesis 11:1–9)

In the days after the great flood, people once again began to spread out and settle across the land. They journeyed east until they found a broad, flat plain in the land of Shinar, where the soil was rich and the ground seemed perfect for building a new life. The people spoke one common language and worked together with remarkable unity.

As they prospered, they began to dream. They decided to build a city unlike any other—a place where they could gather their strength and make a grand name for themselves. At the heart of this plan was a massive tower that would rise into the sky, so tall it would touch the heavens. It would be a monument to human ambition, a way to ensure they would never be scattered across the earth.

They had no stone quarries nearby, so they crafted bricks from clay and baked them hard. Mortar was mixed from tar, thick and black, to bind the bricks together. With determination, they laid brick upon brick. The tower rose steadily, inspiring awe in those who labored on its walls. Yet in their rush to achieve something great, they forgot the true Giver of their abilities.

God looked down upon the city and saw a people consumed with pride, building a monument to their own glory rather than reflecting His. He knew that their unity—fueled by arrogance—would only lead them down a more dangerous path. In His wisdom, He decided to intervene. Suddenly, the workers found themselves unable to understand each other's words. The common language they had once shared fractured into many different tongues. Confusion swept through the construction site. Commands were misheard or misunderstood, and arguments arose where there had been harmony.

Unable to continue the tower or stay organized, the people abandoned the project. They drifted away from Shinar, gathering instead with those who spoke their own new languages. The city they had hoped would bring them fame was left unfinished, a silent warning against the danger of pride.

God's plan still prevailed: humanity would spread out over the earth, as He had intended. The tower stood in partial ruin, a reminder that building on our own glory leads only to confusion and division, while true unity is found in honoring the One who gave us life and purpose.

Reflection for Today

1. Have you ever been tempted to "build your own tower" for attention or praise?

2. How can focusing on God's greatness instead of your own

help you find true unity with others?

Prayer

Lord, help me recognize the times when my pride takes center stage. Teach me to honor You first so that my efforts can bring blessing and unity, not confusion. Amen.

Chapter Six

THE CALL OF ABRAHAM (GENESIS 12:1–9)

Long after the Tower of Babel incident, people scattered into tribes and families, each carving out a life in distant lands. In the region called Ur, there lived a man named Abram. Despite the rich culture, trade, and customs of his homeland, there was a restlessness in his spirit. One day, that restlessness was answered by the clear voice of God:

"Leave your country, your people, and your father's household, and go to the land I will show you. I will make you into a great nation and bless you."

It was a startling directive. Abram had grown up in Ur. He knew its winding streets, bustling marketplaces, and the familiar faces of neighbors. Leaving meant embarking on an uncertain journey, not knowing exactly where this "promised land" might be. It also meant trusting a God who had just begun to reveal Himself to Abram in a personal way. The promise of blessing was immense, but so was the sacrifice.

Yet Abram believed. Gathering his wife Sarai, his nephew Lot, and all their servants and possessions, he set off. Day after day, they traveled across scorching deserts and through unfamiliar territories. The sun beat down on them by day, and at night, they set up camp under the sprawling canopy of stars.

Through windstorms and dusty roads, Abram clung to God's words. Perhaps friends and onlookers found his decision bizarre—risking comfort and security for a vague hope. Still, Abram pressed forward, guided by God's quiet leading. At last, they arrived in the land of Canaan. To any passerby, it might have looked like an ordinary strip of countryside. But God whispered again to Abram, **"To your offspring, I will give this land."**

Moved by gratitude and awe, Abram built an altar there—a simple mound of stones—to honor God. In that moment, amidst a foreign land and uncertain future, Abram's faith was anchored. Though he didn't see how or when God's promise would unfold, he had chosen to trust the One who had called him out. And that trust, as shaky as it might have sometimes felt, would shape the story of God's people for generations to come.

Reflection for Today

1. Have you ever felt God prompting you to step out of your comfort zone without a clear roadmap?

2. What might it look like for you to trust God's leading even when the outcome seems uncertain?

Prayer

Lord, give me the courage to follow Your call wherever it leads. Strengthen my faith when doubts arise, and help me remember that You keep Your promises. Amen.

Chapter Seven

God's Covenant with Abraham (Genesis 15 & 17)

After settling in the land of Canaan, Abram (later renamed Abraham) looked around at the expansive hills and valleys that God had promised him. Though he'd obeyed God's call to leave his homeland, his life didn't become instantly simple or secure. He still had no child to inherit the promise, and with each passing year, the dream of fatherhood seemed further out of reach.

One night, overwhelmed by doubt, Abram poured out his fears to God. He questioned whether all these promises of descendants and blessing could really come true if he had no son. God responded by leading Abram outside into the quiet night sky.

"Look up at the sky and count the stars—if indeed you can count them," God said. **"So shall your offspring be."**

In that moment, Abram lifted his eyes and took in the dazzling spectacle of countless stars shimmering overhead. Something inside him stirred—his faith. He chose to believe that the same God who created those stars could fulfill a promise that seemed impossible. God considered this trust as righteousness, a deep bond of friendship between them.

Later, God formalized this promise with a covenant. He changed Abram's name to Abraham, meaning "father of many," and Sarai's name to Sarah, meaning "princess," as a sign that they were set apart for a divine purpose. Though they were both old, God declared they would have a son within a year. This would be the child through whom generations would arise, forming a nation dedicated to God.

In return, Abraham and his household were to keep the outward sign of this covenant—the practice of circumcision. It symbolized a commitment that went deeper than just a physical mark; it was a sign that Abraham's family belonged to God in a unique, everlasting way.

Decades had slipped by since Abraham first stepped out in faith. He'd navigated doubts, fears, even conflicts. But this covenant felt like a fresh affirmation from God, as if to say, **"I see you, I've not forgotten you, and I will do what I promised."** With renewed confidence, Abraham carried on, eagerly awaiting the miracle that would soon change his life forever.

Reflection for Today

1. When you feel uncertain or impatient, how do you respond to God's promises or guidance?

2. Why do you think God values faith—trusting Him even when circumstances seem impossible?

Prayer

Faithful God, help me to believe Your promises even when doubts cloud my mind. Strengthen my faith, and remind me that You will always keep Your word. Amen.

Chapter Eight

Hagar and Ishmael (Genesis 16; 21:1–21)

Even after God promised Abraham that he would be the father of many nations, years passed and he and his wife, Sarah, still had no child together. Doubt began to gnaw at Sarah's heart. Perhaps she thought God's promise would never be fulfilled in the way she expected. In an attempt to take matters into her own hands, Sarah suggested that Abraham have a child through her Egyptian servant, Hagar, a practice that was culturally acceptable in their day but not aligned with the deeper plan God had in mind.

Hagar conceived, and tension quickly flooded the household. The pregnant servant, feeling elevated by her new status, looked with contempt on her mistress. Hurt and jealous, Sarah treated Hagar harshly, which drove the servant to flee into the desert. Alone and afraid,

Hagar collapsed by a spring of water, tears mixing with the dust. But there, an angel of the Lord appeared to her, calling her by name and gently instructing her to return. He comforted her with the promise that her son, Ishmael, would also become the father of a multitude. Encouraged by God's care, Hagar obeyed, trusting that somehow, she and her child would be safe in Abraham's household.

In time, Hagar gave birth to Ishmael. For many years, he was Abraham's only son. But eventually, God's promise to give Abraham and Sarah a child of their own came to pass. Sarah bore a son, Isaac, in her old age, bringing laughter and joy into their lives. However, the tension within the family did not disappear. When Sarah noticed Ishmael teasing his younger half-brother, her jealousy flared again. Unable to bear the conflict, she insisted that Abraham send Hagar and Ishmael away.

Heartbroken, Abraham packed provisions for them and sent them into the desert. Under the scorching sun, their water soon ran out. Hagar, despairing for her child, placed Ishmael under a bush to shield him from the heat. Then, she moved away, overwhelmed by the thought of watching him die. But once more, God intervened. A voice from heaven reassured Hagar that Ishmael was not forsaken. He opened her eyes to a well of water, reviving their hope and giving them the means to survive. True to His word, God watched over Ishmael as he grew, blessing him to become a strong archer and the ancestor of a great nation.

Though Hagar's story was marked by struggle and displacement, it also shone with God's compassion. From a barren desert to a complicated family dynamic, He saw her tears, heard her cries, and provided for her needs—proving that no one is truly invisible or unloved in His eyes.

Reflection for Today

1. Have you ever taken matters into your own hands instead of waiting on God's timing or guidance?

2. In difficult or lonely moments, how can you remind yourself that God sees you and cares about your needs?

Prayer

God who sees and provides, thank You for caring about me, even when I feel alone or overlooked. Help me trust Your timing and rely on Your compassion. Amen.

Chapter Nine

SODOM AND GOMORRAH (GENESIS 18–19)

Abraham was living by the oaks of Mamre when he received three unexpected visitors. Though they appeared as ordinary travelers, one of them spoke and acted with divine authority. During their visit, Abraham eagerly showed hospitality—rushing to prepare food and water so they could refresh themselves. As they conversed, Abraham learned these guests were on their way to the cities of Sodom and Gomorrah, places infamous for their wickedness and cruelty.

Concerned for any righteous people who might dwell there, Abraham pleaded with the Lord: **"Will you sweep away the righteous with the wicked? What if there are fifty righteous people? What if only ten?"** Abraham's heart ached, knowing his nephew Lot and his family lived in Sodom. Patiently, God assured him that if even ten righteous people could be found in the city, He would spare it.

When two angels arrived in Sodom that evening, Lot welcomed them into his home, offering them a meal and a place to stay. But the men of Sodom, wicked and aggressive, surrounded Lot's house, demanding that the visitors be handed over to them. Horrified, Lot tried to protect his guests, and the angels struck the attackers with blindness, rescuing Lot and his household from immediate danger.

By dawn, the angels urged Lot to flee the city, warning of its impending destruction. They led him, his wife, and two daughters outside the gates, commanding them not to look back. As soon as they reached safety, fire rained down from the heavens, reducing Sodom and Gomorrah to ash. Tragically, Lot's wife disobeyed the angels' warning. She turned to look back at the city she was leaving behind, and in that moment, she became a pillar of salt.

The scene was devastating. Smoke rose in columns where once people had lived in comfort, if not goodness. Yet God's judgment, though severe, underscored His commitment to righteousness and mercy. Abraham, watching from a distance, must have grieved over the loss but taken comfort that his nephew had escaped. This story stands as a stark reminder that when God warns us about the consequences of sin, He does so out of both justice and love.

Reflection for Today

1. Have you ever found it difficult to leave behind something you knew wasn't good for you?

2. How can remembering God's warnings help you make better choices?

Prayer

Just and merciful God, help me to heed Your warnings and stay on the path You've set. Give me courage to walk away from what's harmful and trust in Your love and protection. Amen.

Chapter Ten

THE BIRTH OF ISAAC (GENESIS 21:1–7)

Year after year, Abraham and Sarah had longed for a child. Their tent was often filled with laughter as they welcomed guests or tended their animals, but there was an unspoken ache—a desire for a son or daughter that seemed less likely with every passing day. Still, God's promise lingered in their hearts, a distant but persistent hope.

Then, when both were well beyond the usual age for having children, the unthinkable happened. Sarah became pregnant. In her old age, she carried the precious life that God had promised, each passing month a testament to God's power over the impossible.

Finally, the day arrived. Sarah gave birth to a healthy baby boy. They named him Isaac, which means "he laughs," capturing the blend of astonishment and joy that burst from their hearts. Sarah could hardly believe it. She cradled her infant son, her eyes brimming with happy tears. **"God has brought me laughter,"** she said, **"and everyone who hears about this will laugh with me."**

It was a celebration of life, yes, but also of faith. God's word had not failed. In Isaac, Abraham and Sarah found hope that a new generation would carry on God's covenant, one that would someday expand to bless every family on earth. Though the journey had been marked by doubt, detours, and impatience, at this moment the promise stood fulfilled in the tiny hands and bright eyes of their newborn son.

Reflection for Today

1. Have you ever felt like something was impossible, only to see a breakthrough at just the right time?

2. How do you respond when God's timing doesn't match your expectations?

Prayer

God of miracles, thank You for showing that nothing is beyond Your power. Teach me to wait on Your promises with faith, even when I can't see how they will unfold. Amen.

Chapter Eleven

THE TESTING OF ABRAHAM (GENESIS 22:1–19)

For many years, Abraham and Sarah's life centered around their beloved son, Isaac. Laughter filled their tent whenever the boy ran across the fields or asked curious questions about the world. He was the living proof that God's promises could break through impossibility. Abraham took great delight in teaching Isaac about the God who had blessed their family.

Then, one day, God spoke to Abraham with a command that struck at the very core of his faith: **"Take your son, your only son, whom you love—Isaac—and go to the region of Moriah. Sacrifice him there as a burnt offering on one of the mountains I will show you."** The words were unthinkable, and yet Abraham recognized the voice of God. How could the child of promise be required as a sacrifice?

Despite the heartbreak, Abraham chose to obey. Early the next morning, he rose, saddled his donkey, and took Isaac and two servants on the journey. Each step must have felt heavier than the last, yet Abraham pressed on, trusting that God somehow had a plan. On the third day, he saw the place in the distance—a lonely hill where stones jutted from the ground like silent witnesses.

Abraham told his servants to stay behind while he and Isaac went ahead to worship. Isaac shouldered the bundle of wood while Abraham carried the fire and knife. With childlike innocence, Isaac asked, **"Father, the fire and wood are here, but where is the lamb for the offering?"** Abraham's voice trembled as he answered, **"God Himself will provide the lamb, my son."**

Reaching the summit, Abraham built an altar and laid the wood in place. Then, with deep sorrow, he bound Isaac's hands and placed him upon the altar. Just as he raised the knife, a voice from heaven thundered: **"Do not lay a hand on the boy! Now I know you fear God, because you have not withheld from Me your son."**

In that moment, Abraham looked up and saw a ram caught by its horns in a nearby thicket. Overcome with relief, he offered the ram as the sacrifice instead. Isaac was spared. Shaken but filled with awe, Abraham named the place **"The Lord Will Provide,"** recognizing that God had tested him and shown His faithfulness once again. This event sealed Abraham's faith like nothing else could. God repeated His promise that Abraham's descendants would be as numerous as the stars in the sky, a blessing for all nations.

Reflection for Today

1. When have you faced a situation where obedience to God seemed to contradict your understanding or desires?

2. How can trusting God in difficult circumstances help strengthen your faith?

Prayer

Heavenly Father, give me the courage to trust You even when I don't understand Your ways. Help me to remember that You are faithful and that You provide in every situation. Amen.

Chapter Twelve

Jacob's Dream (Genesis 28:10–22)

Jacob was running from home, fleeing the anger of his older brother, Esau. He'd tricked Esau out of the family blessing through deceit, leaving behind all that was familiar. As the sun dipped below the horizon, Jacob found himself on a lonely stretch of land with nothing but a rock for a pillow. The twilight sky glimmered with distant stars while a cool wind swept across the desert.

That night, as sleep claimed him, Jacob had a vision: a towering ladder stretched from earth all the way up to heaven. Bright, glowing angels were moving up and down its rungs, and at the top stood the Lord Himself. In a voice that resonated like distant thunder yet carried a comforting warmth, God repeated the promise He had once made to Abraham and Isaac: Jacob's descendants would become a great nation, and all peoples of the earth would be blessed through them. Moreover,

God reassured Jacob, **"I am with you and will watch over you wherever you go."**

Jacob awoke with a gasp, heart pounding as he recalled the awe-inspiring sight. In the gray light of dawn, he realized that this barren patch of ground was in fact a sacred place, touched by the presence of the Almighty. Stunned, he exclaimed, **"Surely the Lord is in this place, and I was not aware of it."**

He took the stone he'd used as a pillow and set it upright, pouring oil on its surface. This was an act of devotion—a way to mark the spot and dedicate it to God. He named the place Bethel, which means "House of God," vowing that if the Lord would indeed protect him and provide for him, then Jacob would commit himself fully to worshiping and honoring God.

Though Jacob's journey was far from over, this encounter changed him. The promise that God had not abandoned him—despite his mistakes, his fears, and his uncertainty—sparked a new kind of hope. That rocky campsite in the middle of nowhere became a reminder that no situation is truly deserted when God is present.

Reflection for Today

1. Have you ever felt alone or uncertain, only to discover that God was working behind the scenes?

2. In what practical ways can you acknowledge God's presence in your everyday life?

Prayer

God who meets us in unexpected places, thank You for never leaving us, even when we feel lost or afraid. Help me to trust Your promises and follow You with a devoted heart. Amen.

Chapter Thirteen

JOSEPH SOLD INTO SLAVERY (GENESIS 37)

Jacob's favorite son was Joseph, a dreamer with a heart full of curiosity. Unlike his older brothers, he received a special coat from their father—a richly colored garment that spoke of favor and love. Whenever Joseph walked by wearing that coat, his brothers' eyes burned with envy. It didn't help that Joseph often shared grand dreams in which he seemed destined to rise above them all.

One day, Jacob sent Joseph to check on his brothers, who were tending the family's flocks in a distant pasture. Joseph dutifully obeyed, setting out across the rolling hills and rugged terrain. But when the brothers saw him coming in the distance, they seethed with resentment. **"Here comes that dreamer,"** they muttered. Tired of feeling overshadowed, they hatched a cruel plan.

At first, they thought to kill Joseph and be done with him. But the oldest brother, Reuben, urged them not to shed blood. Instead, they stripped Joseph of his prized coat and threw him into a dry cistern, a pit in the ground once used for storing water. Joseph's pleas echoed off the dusty walls, but their anger dulled any sense of compassion.

While they ate a meal nearby, a caravan of Midianite traders appeared, heading toward Egypt with spices and goods. Another brother, Judah, suggested they profit from Joseph's misfortune. So they hauled him up out of the pit and sold him for twenty pieces of silver. The boy who had once worn a bright cloak of favor was now bound and led away as a slave.

To deceive their father, the brothers tore Joseph's coat and dipped it in goat's blood. Later, when they presented it to Jacob, he broke down in grief, convinced a wild animal had devoured his beloved son.

Meanwhile, Joseph's world had completely changed. He must have wondered if he would ever see his family again, if the dreams God had given him were now doomed to fade into nothing. Little did he know that this betrayal, as painful as it was, would be the first step in a greater plan—one that would eventually save many lives, including his own family's.

Reflection for Today

1. Have you ever experienced jealousy in your own life—either as the one envying someone else or being envied?

2. How might difficult or painful events sometimes be part of a bigger plan that we can't yet see?

Prayer

God, when I face betrayal or envy—whether from others or within my own heart—help me to trust that You can bring purpose from pain. Teach me to respond with patience and faith, believing You hold my future. Amen.

Chapter Fourteen

Joseph in Egypt (Genesis 39–41)

Sold as a slave, Joseph entered Egypt full of uncertainty. He found himself purchased by Potiphar, an influential Egyptian official. It was a daunting new life—far from his family and everything familiar. Yet, despite the heartbreak and betrayal, Joseph held fast to the knowledge that God was still with him. He worked diligently, refusing to let bitterness take hold of his heart.

Before long, Potiphar noticed something remarkable about Joseph: every task Joseph touched seemed to prosper. Whether it was organizing household supplies or managing laborers, Joseph proved both capable and trustworthy. Over time, Potiphar promoted him to oversee his entire household. It was a position of significant responsibility and respect, especially for someone who began as a foreign slave.

But trouble soon loomed. Potiphar's wife took an improper interest in Joseph. Day after day, she tried to lure him into wrongdoing.

Joseph refused, knowing such a betrayal would wound Potiphar's trust and dishonor God. Finally, when Joseph still rejected her advances, she falsely accused him of assault. Furious and humiliated, Potiphar had Joseph thrown into prison.

Prison was a harsh and hopeless place, but again Joseph chose faith over despair. He helped fellow inmates and served the prison warden faithfully. God's favor rested on him even in those dark cells; soon, the warden trusted him with administrative duties, watching over other prisoners and running daily routines.

Among Joseph's fellow inmates were two former officials of Pharaoh: his cupbearer and his baker. Both had disturbing dreams they couldn't interpret. Joseph, giving credit to God as the true interpreter, asked them to share their visions. He told the cupbearer he would soon be restored to his position, but warned the baker that his fate would be grim. Within days, both interpretations proved accurate.

As the cupbearer prepared to return to Pharaoh's court, Joseph pleaded, **"Remember me and mention me to Pharaoh, so I can get out of this prison."** The cupbearer nodded, promising help. But once he was free, the busy days of palace life made him forget about the young Hebrew in prison.

Two years passed. Joseph remained behind bars, faithfully doing his duties and waiting on God. One night, Pharaoh was tormented by dreams of seven healthy cows followed by seven scrawny, sickly cows—and again of seven plump heads of grain devoured by seven withered heads. No one in the kingdom could interpret these nightmares. Suddenly, the cupbearer remembered Joseph's gift. Rushing to Pharaoh, he confessed that he knew of a man who had correctly interpreted dreams.

Immediately, Pharaoh summoned Joseph. After shaving and dressing in clean clothes, Joseph stood before the most powerful ruler in Egypt. **"I hear you can interpret dreams,"** Pharaoh said. Joseph humbly answered, **"I cannot do it, but God will give Pharaoh the answer he desires."**

Listening carefully to Pharaoh's account of the dreams, Joseph explained: there would be seven years of abundant harvests in Egypt, followed by seven years of devastating famine. **"Select a wise and discerning man,"** Joseph advised, **"to store up grain during the years of plenty so there will be food in the years of famine."**

Impressed by Joseph's insight and integrity, Pharaoh declared, **"Can we find anyone like this man, one in whom is the spirit of God?"** He appointed Joseph second-in-command over all Egypt. Joseph was given royal robes, Pharaoh's signet ring, and authority to carry out his plan. Through God's guidance, Joseph would manage the stockpiling of grain so that countless lives—including his own family—would eventually be saved from starvation.

Reflection for Today

1. Have you ever felt overlooked or forgotten, even though you were doing the right thing?

2. How can trusting God's timing and plan change your attitude during long periods of waiting?

Prayer

Lord, thank You for the reminder that You are always at work, even when our situation feels hopeless. Help me trust Your plan and remain faithful, knowing that in due time You will bring about good. Amen.

Chapter Fifteen

Joseph Reunites with His Family (Genesis 42–50)

Years had passed since Joseph became second-in-command in Egypt. By carefully storing grain during the plentiful years, he had ensured that the nation—and surrounding regions—had food during the ensuing famine. The drought was so severe that even distant lands felt the pangs of hunger.

Far away in Canaan, Joseph's father, Jacob, heard rumors that Egypt was the only place with grain. Desperate, he sent ten of

Joseph's older brothers to buy food, never imagining they would come face-to-face with the sibling they'd betrayed. When the brothers arrived, they bowed low before the governor of the land, not recognizing that this powerful Egyptian official was their own brother. Joseph, however, knew them immediately. Memories flooded his mind: the pit, the silver coins, the jeers. Instead of revealing himself, Joseph tested them to see if they had changed.

He accused them of being spies, demanding they return with their youngest brother, Benjamin, to prove their honesty. Afraid yet determined, the brothers went home and explained the strange situation. Though it grieved him deeply, Jacob agreed to let Benjamin go, praying for God's protection.

When the brothers returned with Benjamin, Joseph secretly arranged a final test. He had a valuable silver cup hidden in Benjamin's sack. Then he accused Benjamin of theft. Under this fresh accusation, one of the brothers—Judah—stepped forward, offering himself as a slave in place of Benjamin. This act of self-sacrifice was exactly what Joseph needed to see. Moved to tears, he cleared the room of attendants and revealed his true identity: **"I am Joseph, your brother!"**

The brothers were speechless, terrified at how Joseph might punish them for their past cruelty. But Joseph, overwhelmed by compassion, reassured them. **"You meant evil against me, but God used it for good—to save many lives."** He embraced them, weeping with joy. All the resentment and fear of the past melted away in that moment of forgiveness.

Soon, Joseph sent for his father. The entire family uprooted from Canaan and settled in Goshen, a region in Egypt where they could survive the famine under Joseph's protection. Jacob, now an old man, was overcome with gratitude and relief. He had believed for years that

Joseph was dead. Yet here he was, alive and exalted, ensuring not just the family's survival but its thriving.

In time, Jacob passed away, and Joseph's brothers worried he might finally seek revenge. But Joseph's heart remained gracious. **"Am I in the place of God?"** he asked them gently. **"Don't be afraid."** He continued to care for them, living out the truth that God's plans can transform even the darkest betrayals into instruments of blessing.

Reflection for Today

1. Have you ever struggled to forgive someone who hurt you deeply? What might Joseph's story teach you?

2. How can difficult events in your life—whether caused by others or by circumstance—be used for a greater purpose?

Prayer

Merciful God, thank You for showing us how forgiveness can bring healing. Help me to trust that You can bring good out of bad situations and teach me to offer the same grace You've shown me. Amen.

Chapter Sixteen

Moses and the Burning Bush (Exodus 3–4)

Many years after Joseph's family settled in Egypt, a new Pharaoh rose to power who no longer remembered Joseph or the help he had provided. Threatened by the growing numbers of the Israelite people, this Pharaoh enslaved them under harsh conditions. In that oppressive climate, a Hebrew baby named Moses was born—destined for a remarkable path. Through a series of dramatic events, he was adopted by Pharaoh's daughter but later fled Egypt after defending a fellow Hebrew.

Far from the wealth and splendor of the palace, Moses found himself in the rugged wilderness of Midian, tending sheep for his father-in-law. Day after dusty day, he led the flock across rocky terrain, searching for pasture and water. Life had settled into a humble rhythm, miles away from his troubled past.

Then, in the quiet of a desert afternoon, Moses noticed something extraordinary: a bush engulfed in flames yet not burning up. Intrigued, he drew closer. Suddenly, a voice called out from the fire, **"Moses! Moses!"** Startled, he replied, **"Here I am."**

The voice identified itself as the God of Abraham, Isaac, and Jacob—the God of Moses' ancestors. **"Take off your sandals,"** God commanded, **"for the place where you are standing is holy ground."** Reverently, Moses slipped off his sandals. Awe, fear, and wonder collided in his heart.

God revealed that He had seen the suffering of the Israelites in Egypt, and He had chosen Moses to lead them out of captivity. Moses was overwhelmed. Memories of his past failures surged in his mind. In disbelief, he asked, **"Who am I that I should go to Pharaoh?"** But God's assurance rang clear: **"I will be with you."**

Still, Moses was reluctant. He feared the Israelites would doubt his calling. **"What if they ask Your name?"** he asked. God replied, **"I AM WHO I AM. Tell them 'I AM' has sent you."**

Despite this revelation, Moses still wrestled with insecurity. He pointed out his poor speaking ability, afraid of addressing Pharaoh and the Hebrew people. Patiently, God provided signs to confirm Moses' authority—turning his staff into a snake and then back again, and making his hand become leprous and then healed. Finally, God agreed to send Moses' brother, Aaron, to help speak on his behalf.

At last, Moses yielded. He left the burning bush forever changed, carrying with him the conviction that the God of his ancestors was both holy and compassionate. The old life of shepherding in Midian was over. A new chapter began—one in which Moses would confront the most powerful ruler in the land, armed not with sword or spear, but with God's own presence and promise.

Reflection for Today

> 1. Have you ever felt that God was calling you to do something beyond your abilities or comfort zone?

> 2. How can remembering "God is with me" help you overcome fear or self-doubt?

Prayer

Lord, thank You for meeting me in unexpected places and calling me to step out in faith. Help me trust that You are always with me, equipping me for whatever You ask me to do. Amen.

Chapter Seventeen

THE PLAGUES AND THE PASSOVER (EXODUS 7–12)

At God's command, Moses returned to Egypt with his brother Aaron. Their mission was daunting: persuade Pharaoh to release the Israelites from slavery. But the proud king's heart was hardened. He saw no reason to obey a God he didn't know, especially if it meant losing his entire workforce.

So Moses and Aaron performed the signs God had given them. Aaron threw down his staff, and it became a snake; Pharaoh's magicians mimicked the trick with their own staffs, but their snakes were devoured by Aaron's. Yet Pharaoh remained unmoved.

Then came the plagues, each a demonstration of God's power and a direct challenge to Egypt's false gods:

1. **Water to Blood:** The Nile—lifeblood of the na-

tion—turned crimson. Fish died, and the waters reeked. Still, Pharaoh's heart remained cold.

2. **Frogs:** A horde of slimy frogs invaded homes, beds, and cooking pots. Pharaoh begged for relief but changed his mind once the frogs were gone.

3. **Gnats:** Dust transformed into swarms of tiny insects, pestering people and animals. Even Pharaoh's magicians recognized **"this is the finger of God,"** but the king refused to listen.

4. **Flies:** Clouds of flies tormented the land, but God spared the region where the Israelites lived.

5. **Livestock Disease:** Egyptian cattle, horses, and donkeys perished, yet Israelite animals remained healthy.

6. **Boils:** Painful sores afflicted Egyptians and their beasts, but Pharaoh's heart still did not soften.

7. **Hail:** A storm of thunder and ice rained down, destroying crops and fields. Pharaoh briefly pretended to repent, but reneged once the hail stopped.

8. **Locusts:** Swarms of hungry insects devoured whatever greenery remained. Egypt's once-fertile landscape was reduced to ruin.

9. **Darkness:** For three days, an oppressive blackness covered the land—so thick that lamps seemed useless. Even then, Pharaoh would not fully let the Hebrews go.

Finally, God warned of a tenth and final plague: the death of every firstborn in Egypt. To protect the Israelites, He instructed each Hebrew family to sacrifice a spotless lamb and smear its blood on their doorposts. That night, God's judgment passed through Egypt. Where there was no lamb's blood on the door, the firstborn child died.

In the middle of the night, a great cry rose in Egypt. Even Pharaoh's own firstborn son lay lifeless. Broken by grief, Pharaoh commanded Moses and Aaron to take their people and leave immediately.

Yet, for the Israelites, the night of mourning became a moment of salvation. Every household with the lamb's blood marking its door was spared. The meal they had eaten—the roasted lamb, unleavened bread, and bitter herbs—became the foundation of the Passover feast. From that day forward, God's people would celebrate Passover each year, remembering how God saved them from slavery and death.

With hearts both sobered and hopeful, the Israelites packed their belongings and set out. They carried with them more than physical possessions; they carried the memory of God's mighty power and the promise of freedom He had secured on their behalf.

Reflection for Today

1. Have you ever witnessed or experienced a situation that reminded you there's a power higher than any human authority?

2. In what ways can remembering God's past faithfulness give you hope for your present challenges?

Prayer

God of deliverance, thank You for reminding me that no power on earth compares to Yours. Help me trust Your plan in difficult times, and may I never forget how You bring freedom from fear and bondage. Amen.

Chapter Eighteen

Crossing the Red Sea (Exodus 14)

After the night of the final plague, the Israelites fled Egypt in a rush, following Moses into the wilderness. Their hearts were full of relief and amazement—God had broken Pharaoh's iron grip. But as they journeyed, Pharaoh's grief turned to fury. Determined not to lose his entire workforce, he rallied his chariots and armies and set off in hot pursuit.

The Israelites soon found themselves trapped: in front of them lay the vast Red Sea, and behind them thundered Pharaoh's chariots. Panic gripped the people. **"Why did you bring us out here to die?"** some complained to Moses. Fear weighed heavily, threatening to snuff out the flicker of hope they had carried.

In that desperate moment, Moses spoke with unshakeable faith: **"Do not be afraid. Stand firm, and you will see the deliverance the Lord will bring you today. The Egyptians you see today you**

will never see again." As he lifted his staff over the waters, God sent a strong east wind that blew across the sea all night. Miraculously, the Red Sea divided, towering walls of water forming on each side, and the Israelites walked across on dry ground.

Pharaoh's army charged in after them, their horses and chariots racing into the parted seabed. But as dawn broke, the Lord caused confusion among the Egyptians. Wheels jammed and chaos erupted. Once the last Israelite was safely on the far shore, Moses stretched his hand over the sea again. The waters thundered back into place, swallowing Pharaoh's formidable army in a single, crushing wave.

Stunned and overjoyed, the Israelites realized the magnitude of their salvation. With the oppressors gone, they were truly free. Standing on the shore, they lifted their voices in celebration. Moses' sister, Miriam, took up a tambourine, and the people broke into song: **"Sing to the Lord, for He is highly exalted!"** From that day forward, the Red Sea crossing would stand as a defining moment—proof that, no matter how impossible the situation, God's power could make a way where none existed.

Reflection for Today

1. When you feel trapped by fear or circumstance, how can trusting God open a way forward that you couldn't see before?

2. Why do you think it's important to remember and celebrate times when God has rescued or helped you?

Prayer

Mighty God, thank You for being my deliverer when I feel cornered or afraid. Remind me that You can make a path where I see none, and help me to praise You for every victory, large or small. Amen.

Chapter Nineteen

GOD PROVIDES MANNA (EXODUS 16)

After the miraculous crossing of the Red Sea, the Israelites began their journey through the vast wilderness toward the Promised Land. Despite their dramatic escape from Egypt, the challenges of the desert soon became apparent. Days turned into weeks, and the people started to grumble and complain about the scarcity of food and water. They missed the abundance they had known in Egypt and began to question whether God had truly brought them to freedom.

One morning, as the sun cast its first golden rays over the arid landscape, Moses heard the murmurs of discontent rising from the camp. The people were upset, fearing that they had made a terrible mistake by leaving behind the security of Egypt. They begged Moses, **"If only we had died by the hand of the Lord in Egypt! There we sat around pots of meat and ate all the food we wanted, but** you have brought us out into this desert to starve this entire assembly to death."

Moses turned to the Lord in frustration, seeking guidance on how to satisfy the people's hunger. God responded with a clear directive: **"I will rain down bread from heaven for you. The people are to go out each day and gather enough for that day. In this way, I will test them and see whether they will follow my instructions."**

That night, as Moses relayed God's message to the people, a sense of hope began to replace their fear. The next morning, dew covered the desert floor, and as the sun rose, small, flaky flakes began to fall from the sky. The Israelites watched in awe as God provided them with manna—bread from heaven. Each person gathered just enough for their needs, and there was no waste. When the people asked Moses, **"What are we to eat?"** he replied, **"The Lord has given you the Sabbath; the day before the Sabbath, you will gather twice as much manna."**

This miraculous provision continued for forty years, sustaining the Israelites as they journeyed through the wilderness. Manna became a daily reminder of God's faithfulness and His ability to provide for His people's needs, even in the most unlikely circumstances. It taught them to trust in God's provision and to rely on Him daily, fostering a deeper sense of dependence and gratitude.

As the Israelites learned to gather and cherish the manna, they also received laws and instructions from God, laying the foundation for their identity as His chosen people. The daily bread was not just physical sustenance but also a symbol of God's ongoing care and the covenant relationship He maintained with them.

Reflection for Today

1. When have you had to rely on God for daily needs or unexpected challenges?

2. How can practicing gratitude for what you receive each day deepen your relationship with God?

Prayer

Provider God, thank You for meeting my needs each day, even when I feel uncertain or overwhelmed. Help me to trust in Your provision and to cultivate a heart of gratitude for all that You give. Amen.

Chapter Twenty

THE TEN COMMANDMENTS (EXODUS 19–20)

After the miraculous escape from Egypt and the dramatic crossing of the Red Sea, the Israelites journeyed into the wilderness, led by Moses. They camped at Mount Sinai, a majestic peak that touched the heavens, symbolizing the profound encounter that was about to unfold. The air was thick with anticipation as the people settled in, aware that something extraordinary was about to happen.

Three days before the appointed day, God spoke to Moses in a powerful voice, sending thunder, lightning, and thick clouds that covered the mountain. The sound of the trumpet grew louder and more intense, and the mountain trembled with divine presence. The people stood at a distance, watching in awe and fear as smoke billowed from the summit, making it appear as if the mountain was ablaze.

Moses ascended the mountain to speak with God, leaving the people to wait below. On the third day, amidst the roar of thunder and the flash of lightning, God delivered His commandments directly to the Israelites. These were not just rules but foundational principles meant to guide their relationship with Him and with one another.

The Ten Commandments were etched on two stone tablets, each inscribed with God's own words:

1. **You shall have no other gods before Me.**

2. **You shall not make for yourself an idol.**

3. **You shall not misuse the name of the Lord your God.**

4. **Remember the Sabbath day by keeping it holy.**

5. **Honor your father and your mother.**

6. **You shall not murder.**

7. **You shall not commit adultery.**

8. **You shall not steal.**

9. **You shall not give false testimony against your neighbor.**

10. **You shall not covet anything that belongs to your neighbor.**

These commandments established a moral and ethical framework that was revolutionary for the time. They emphasized the importance of worshiping God exclusively, maintaining integrity, honoring family, and fostering a just and compassionate community.

As the people listened, their fear began to transform into reverence and understanding. They recognized the gravity of God's laws and the sacredness of their covenant relationship with Him. Moses, acting as the mediator, communicated God's expectations clearly, ensuring that the Israelites knew how to live in a way that honored their God and upheld their community's well-being.

The giving of the Ten Commandments was a pivotal moment for the Israelites. It solidified their identity as God's chosen people, committed to living by His standards. These commandments were not merely restrictions but expressions of God's love and desire for His people to thrive in harmony and righteousness.

Reflection for Today

1. How do the Ten Commandments influence the way you interact with God and others in your daily life?

2. Which of the commandments do you find most challenging to follow, and why?

Prayer

Lord, thank You for Your guidance and the principles You've set for us to live by. Help me to honor and follow Your commandments, strengthening my relationship with You and with those around me. Amen.

Chapter Twenty-One
The Widow's Oil Miracle (2 Kings 4:1-7)

In a time of widespread famine, a widow of a prophet found herself in desperate circumstances. Her husband had died, leaving her with a large debt to be paid by her late husband's creditor. Without the means to repay, her only option was to sell her two sons to the creditor as servants. In her distress, the widow sought Elisha's help, pleading for a miracle to save her family from this dire fate.

Elisha responded with a message of hope: **"Go, sell the oil jars and make your sons a heap. Pour from them, and fill all the vessels to the brim."** The widow, although uncertain, trusted the prophet and followed his instructions. She began by collecting as many empty jars as she could from her neighbors, creating a large pile.

As she poured her small amount of olive oil into the jars, a miraculous transformation occurred. The oil kept flowing, filling jar after jar until there were no empty vessels left. The widow's debt was paid in full, and she and her sons were spared from being sold. This miracle not only provided for her immediate needs but also restored her faith in God's provision.

The Widow's Oil Miracle is a powerful story of faith, obedience, and God's ability to provide abundantly in times of need. It teaches us that even when resources seem scarce, trusting in God's guidance can lead to extraordinary outcomes.

Reflection for Today

1. **Have you ever been in a situation where you had to rely on faith and obedience despite uncertainty? What was the outcome?**

2. **How can you cultivate trust in God's provision when facing financial or personal challenges?**

Short Prayer

Provider God, thank You for the unwavering faith this story teaches. Help me to trust in Your guidance and provision, especially when circumstances seem dire. Grant me the courage to act in faith, knowing that You can transform my limited resources into abundant blessings. Amen.

Chapter Twenty-Two

SAMSON'S STRENGTH (JUDGES 13–16)

In the time of the Judges, when Israel was frequently oppressed by neighboring nations, the story of Samson emerged as one of both incredible strength and profound weakness. Samson was born to a barren woman, Manoah's wife, as a result of an angelic visitation. The angel announced that Samson was to be a Nazirite from birth, meaning he was set apart for God's service. This dedication included abstaining from alcohol, avoiding contact with the dead, and not cutting his hair—a symbol of his vow to God.

From a young age, Samson displayed extraordinary physical strength. His feats were legendary: he single-handedly killed a lion, defeated an entire army with just the jawbone of a donkey, and brought down the temple of the Philistines, sacrificing himself to save his people. However, despite his divine calling and remarkable abilities, Samson struggled with personal weaknesses, particularly his vulnerability to temptation and his inability to maintain consistent obedience to God's commands.

One of the most pivotal moments in Samson's life was his relationship with Delilah, a woman from the Philistine city of Sorek. The Philistines, desperate to discover the secret of his strength, bribed Delilah to uncover the source of his power. Delilah persistently coaxed Samson into revealing that his strength lay in his uncut hair. After several failed attempts where Samson misled her or fell asleep, he finally confessed the truth. While he slept, Delilah had his hair cut, breaking his Nazirite vow and leaving him vulnerable.

With his strength gone, the Philistines captured Samson, gouged out his eyes, and imprisoned him. Yet, even in his darkest moments, Samson's story did not end in despair. As his hair began to grow back, he prayed to God for one final act of strength to avenge his blindness and deliver Israel from Philistine oppression. Standing between two pillars of the Philistine temple, Samson pushed against them with all his might, causing the building to collapse. This ultimate sacrifice resulted in the death of many Philistines and fulfilled his role as a judge who delivered Israel, but it also marked the tragic end of a man who could have been a greater instrument of God's will had he fully embraced his calling.

Samson's life is a complex tapestry of divine empowerment and personal failings. His story serves as a powerful lesson on the importance of unwavering faith, the dangers of yielding to temptation, and the profound mercy of God, who can redeem even the most flawed individuals for His purposes.

Reflection for Today

1. Have you ever felt torn between following your strengths and

succumbing to temptations? How can Samson's story help you navigate these struggles?

2. In moments of weakness or failure, how can you seek God's strength to overcome and fulfill your purpose?

Prayer

Heavenly Father, thank You for the lessons from Samson's life. Help me to recognize my own strengths and weaknesses, and to seek Your guidance in overcoming temptations. Empower me to fulfill the purpose You have for me, even when I stumble. Amen.

Chapter Twenty-Three

RUTH AND BOAZ (RUTH)

The story of Ruth is one of loyalty, love, and redemption set against the backdrop of hardship and loss. During a time of famine, Naomi, her husband, and their two sons moved from Bethlehem to the land of Moab in search of sustenance. Tragically, Naomi lost her husband and both sons, leaving her with her two Moabite daughters-in-law: Orpah and Ruth.

Naomi decided to return to Bethlehem, hoping to find a better future. She urged her daughters-in-law to remain in Moab and remarry, but Ruth clung to Naomi with unwavering devotion. **"Where you go, I will go,"** Ruth declared, **"and where you stay, I will stay. Your people will be my people and your God my God."** Her steadfast loyalty and faithfulness set her apart, embodying a deep commitment that would change her destiny.

Upon returning to Bethlehem, Naomi faced the harsh reality of poverty. She encouraged Ruth to seek work in the fields, where she could glean leftover grain to support them. Ruth obediently went to work in the fields of Boaz, a wealthy and kind landowner who was also a relative of Naomi's late husband. Boaz noticed Ruth's diligence and compassion, especially towards Naomi, and he treated her with generosity and respect.

Naomi, recognizing Boaz as a potential redeemer—a relative who could marry Ruth to preserve the family line—strategized to bring them together. She guided Ruth to approach Boaz with humility and grace, requesting his protection and blessing. Boaz was moved by Ruth's integrity and kindness. He ensured that she was well taken care of and promised to fulfill his duty as her redeemer.

However, there was a closer relative who had the first right to redeem Ruth. In a formal meeting at the town gate, Boaz publicly declared his intention to marry Ruth, surpassing the other relative. Their union was blessed by God, bringing joy and restoration to Naomi's family. Ruth and Boaz had a son named Obed, who became the grandfather of King David, placing Ruth directly in the lineage of Jesus Christ.

Ruth's story is a testament to the power of loyalty, the beauty of loving-kindness, and the way God can orchestrate relationships to fulfill His greater plan. Her journey from a foreign widow to the great-grandmother of a king illustrates how faith and integrity can lead to unexpected blessings and divine purposes.

Reflection for Today

1. How can Ruth's loyalty and commitment inspire you in your relationships and friendships?

2. In what ways can you show kindness and integrity in your daily interactions, even when it's challenging?

Prayer

Gracious God, thank You for the inspiring story of Ruth and Boaz. Help me to be loyal and kind in my relationships, and to trust that You can bring about wonderful blessings through acts of faithfulness. Guide me to live with integrity and compassion each day. Amen.

Chapter Twenty-Four

Samuel Hears God's Voice (1 Samuel 3)

During a time when Israel lacked a king and was led by judges, the young boy Samuel served faithfully in the temple under the priest Eli. Though Samuel was dedicated to God, he struggled to understand the spiritual decline happening among the people of Israel, as they drifted away from their covenant with God.

One night, as Samuel lay down to sleep in the tabernacle, he heard a voice calling his name. Thinking it was Eli, he ran to the priest and exclaimed, **"Here I am; you called me."** But Eli had not called him. This happened three times, and each time Samuel went to Eli, only to be told, **"Go and lie down, and if he calls you, say, 'Speak, Lord, for your servant is listening.'"**

After the third call, Eli realized that it was God who was calling Samuel. He instructed Samuel on how to respond, teaching him to acknowledge God's voice and to listen attentively. When the voice called again, Samuel followed Eli's guidance. This time, God shared a message of judgment, announcing that He would punish Eli's family for the unfaithfulness of Eli's sons, who had corrupted the priestly duties.

Though the message was harsh, Samuel received it with obedience and courage. He became a trusted prophet of God, leading the Israelites back to faithfulness. This pivotal moment marked the beginning of Samuel's prophetic ministry and his significant role in guiding Israel during a critical period.

Samuel's experience of hearing and responding to God's call highlights the importance of listening for God's voice, the need for guidance in discerning His will, and the courage required to act on His commands. It serves as a powerful reminder that God speaks to us in various ways and that we must be attentive and ready to respond with faith and obedience.

Reflection for Today

1. Have you ever felt a calling or sensed that God was speaking to you? How did you respond?

2. What can you do to become more attentive to God's voice in your daily life?

Short Prayer

Dear Lord, thank You for speaking to me in ways I might not always recognize. Help me to listen attentively and respond with obedience and faith. Guide me to discern Your voice and follow Your will in all that I do. Amen.

Chapter Twenty-Five

DAVID AND GOLIATH (1 SAMUEL 17)

In the early days of Israel's monarchy, the young shepherd David stood out not just for his faith but also for his remarkable courage. While serving his father Jesse's flock, David was sent to the battlefield to deliver food to his brothers, who were fighting against the Philistines. There, he witnessed the towering Philistine warrior, Goliath, challenging the Israelite army to single combat. Goliath's intimidating presence and mocking taunts struck fear into the hearts of the soldiers, who were paralyzed by his size and strength.

David, though only a youth, was appalled by Goliath's defiance of the living God. Unlike the seasoned soldiers, he was not intimidated by physical might; his confidence stemmed from his unwavering trust in God. Declaring that the battle was the Lord's, David volunteered to face Goliath, despite King Saul's doubts and attempts to equip him with armor and weapons that felt foreign to him.

Armed with nothing but his sling and five smooth stones, David approached Goliath with boldness. The giant mocked him, cursing David and his God. Undeterred, David proclaimed that while Goliath came with sword, spear, and javelin, he came in the name of the Lord Almighty. With precise aim, David slung a stone that struck Goliath in the forehead, causing the Philistine warrior to fall face down to the ground. Using Goliath's own sword, David then beheaded him, securing a decisive victory for Israel.

David's triumph over Goliath became a defining moment in his life, showcasing that true strength lies not in physical prowess but in faith and reliance on God. This story inspired the Israelites, lifting their spirits and leading to the Philistines' defeat. It also set the stage for David's rise as a leader and future king of Israel, revered for his heart after God.

The battle between David and Goliath teaches that no challenge is too great when faced with faith, that courage can come from the least expected places, and that God empowers those who trust in Him to overcome seemingly insurmountable obstacles.

Reflection for Today

1. What "giants" are you facing in your life, and how can faith help you overcome them?

2. How can you rely on God's strength instead of your own when confronted with difficult challenges?

Prayer

Brave God, thank You for reminding me that with You, I can face any challenge. Help me to trust in Your strength and courageously confront the giants in my life. Empower me to rely on Your power rather than my own, knowing that You are always by my side. Amen.

Chapter Twenty-Six

David's Heart for God (2 Samuel 6)

King David, renowned for his heart after God, played a pivotal role in establishing Jerusalem as the spiritual and political center of Israel. His deep love for God was evident in every aspect of his life, from his humble beginnings as a shepherd to his celebrated victories as a warrior and leader.

One of the most significant moments that showcased David's devotion was the transportation of the Ark of the Covenant to Jerusalem. The Ark, representing the very presence of God among His people, had been residing in the house of Abinadab in Kiriath-Jearim. David desired to bring the Ark to the heart of Israel, to the city that would become the capital and the center of worship.

David's plan was meticulous and heartfelt. He instructed the Levites, a tribe dedicated to religious duties, to carry the Ark on new carts, led by twelve thousand men with singing and playing musical instruments. The procession was joyous and exuberant, filled with dancing, singing, and celebration. David himself was dancing with all his might before the Lord, his zeal for God apparent to all who witnessed.

However, the event was not without tragedy. As the Ark was being moved, Uzzah, one of the men tasked with guiding the Ark, reached out his hand to steady it when the oxen stumbled. In doing so, he touched the holy Ark, which was strictly forbidden. God's anger burned against Uzzah, and he was struck dead on the spot. This sudden and harsh judgment left David and the people of Israel in mourning, highlighting the holiness of God and the seriousness of approaching Him with reverence.

Despite the sorrow, David did not abandon his mission. He learned the importance of obedience and reverence in worship. Undeterred by the tragedy, David continued to lead the Ark to Jerusalem, ensuring it was placed in a place of honor. His persistent devotion eventually led to the Ark's successful relocation, symbolizing God's enduring presence and favor upon Israel.

David's relationship with God was marked by deep faith, sincere worship, and a relentless pursuit of God's will. His life teaches us about the importance of honoring God with our actions, the need for reverence in worship, and the transformative power of a heart dedicated to seeking and serving God.

Reflection for Today

1. How does David's passion for worship inspire you to honor God in your own life?

2. What lessons can you learn from the incident with Uzzah

about approaching God with reverence and obedience?

Prayer

Loving God, thank You for David's example of a heart fully devoted to You. Help me to worship You with all my might and to approach Your presence with the reverence it deserves. Guide me to honor You in all that I do and to seek Your will above my own. Amen.

Chapter Twenty-Seven

Solomon's Wisdom (1 Kings 3)

As Israel transitioned from a period of judges to a monarchy, Solomon, the son of King David, ascended to the throne. Despite his youth, Solomon was known for his deep love and respect for God, having witnessed his father's devotion. Early in his reign, Solomon faced the daunting task of governing a nation with diverse needs and challenges. Recognizing the magnitude of his responsibilities, he sought divine guidance above all else.

One night, Solomon offered a heartfelt prayer at Gibeon, the location of the Lord's tabernacle. **"Give me wisdom and knowledge,"** he pleaded, **"so I may govern your people effectively and discern right from wrong." "It is you who have shown great mercy,"** Solomon continued, **"by loving your people Israel and by giving me a right heart to govern them."** He concluded by asking God to ensure that he would walk in obedience to His commands so that he might be a wise and just ruler.

God was pleased with Solomon's request, as it demonstrated humility and a genuine desire to lead with righteousness. Instead of long life, riches, or the death of his enemies, God granted Solomon unparalleled wisdom. **"Since this was your request and you have not asked for yourself wealth or honor,"** God declared, **"nor have you asked for the death of your enemies, but for discernment in administering justice, I will do what you have asked. I will give you a wise and discerning heart, so that there will never have been anyone like you, nor will there ever be."**

Solomon's wisdom was soon put to the test. When two women came to him, each claiming to be the mother of the same baby, Solomon proposed to cut the child in half, giving each woman half. The true mother immediately renounced her claim, willing to give up her child to save its life. Recognizing her selfless love, Solomon declared her the rightful mother and spared the child. This wise judgment amazed the people and solidified Solomon's reputation as a divinely gifted king.

Under Solomon's reign, Israel experienced a period of unprecedented prosperity, peace, and cultural flourishing. He built the magnificent Temple in Jerusalem, a place of worship that stood as a testament to Israel's faith and dedication to God. Solomon's wisdom not only governed his people effectively but also fostered unity and respect among the diverse tribes of Israel.

However, Solomon's later years were marred by his own weaknesses. Influenced by foreign wives and their gods, he turned away from exclusive worship of Yahweh, leading to internal strife and the eventual division of the kingdom after his death. Despite these failings, Solomon's early commitment to seeking God's wisdom remains a powerful example of the blessings that come from prioritizing divine guidance over personal ambition.

Solomon's story underscores the importance of wisdom, humility, and obedience in leadership. It highlights how seeking God's will can lead to remarkable achievements and how neglecting that pursuit can result in downfall, serving as a timeless lesson for leaders and individuals alike.

Reflection for Today

1. How can seeking God's wisdom influence your decisions and leadership roles in school, family, or community?

2. What steps can you take to prioritize your relationship with God to ensure you remain guided by His wisdom?

Prayer

Wise God, thank You for granting Solomon the wisdom he sought. Help me to seek Your guidance in every decision I make and to prioritize my relationship with You above all else. Grant me discernment and humility so that I may lead and live in a way that honors You. Amen.

Chapter Twenty-Eight
Elijah vs. Prophets of Baal (1 Kings 18)

During the reign of King Ahab and his wife Jezebel, Israel had fallen into idolatry, worshiping the false god Baal. The prophets of Baal were numerous, promoting practices that contradicted God's commands. Elijah, a prophet of Yahweh, stood as a lone voice of truth and righteousness in a sea of falsehood.

Elijah was a fearless and fervent believer, determined to turn Israel back to the true God. One day, he confronted King Ahab on Mount Carmel, challenging the prophets of Baal to a dramatic showdown. **"There are 450 prophets of Baal and 400 prophets of Asherah,"** Elijah declared, **"and there is not one prophet of the Lord our God here. Let the Lord, the God of Abraham, Isaac and Israel, prove to us who is God."**

The challenge was set: both Elijah and the prophets of Baal would prepare a sacrifice on separate altars without setting fire to it. The God who answered by fire would be acknowledged as the true God. The prophets of Baal went first, fervently calling on their god to send fire from heaven to consume their sacrifice. They danced, shouted, and even cut themselves with swords and spears in their desperate attempts, but Baal remained silent.

Elijah then took his turn. He repaired the altar of the Lord, placing twelve stones to represent the twelve tribes of Israel. He arranged the wood, cut the bull, and poured water over the sacrifice to make the conditions as challenging as possible. **"Lord, the God of Abraham, Isaac and Israel, let it be known today that you are God in Israel and that I am your servant and have done all these things at your command,"** Elijah prayed. **"Answer me, Lord, answer me, so these people will know that you, Lord, are God, and that you are turning their hearts back again."**

In a powerful display of divine power, fire rained down from heaven, consuming the sacrifice, the wood, the stones, the soil, and even the water in the trench. The people fell prostrate, proclaiming, **"The Lord, he is God! The Lord, he is God!"** Elijah then commanded the people to seize and kill the prophets of Baal, effectively eradicating the false worship that had plagued Israel.

Elijah's victory on Mount Carmel was a profound demonstration of God's supremacy and a turning point for the nation of Israel. It reinvigorated the people's faith and affirmed the power of genuine worship. However, the aftermath also led to personal trials for Elijah, including moments of fear and doubt, reminding us that even those who serve faithfully may face their own struggles.

Elijah's story emphasizes the importance of standing firm in faith, challenging falsehood, and trusting in God's power, even when standing alone against overwhelming opposition.

Reflection for Today

1. Have you ever felt like you were standing alone in your beliefs? How did you handle that situation?

2. How can you actively challenge false beliefs or practices in your environment while maintaining your faith?

Prayer

Almighty God, thank You for Elijah's courage and faithfulness. Help me to stand firm in my beliefs, even when I feel alone. Grant me the strength to challenge what is wrong and the wisdom to trust in Your power and guidance. Amen.

Chapter Twenty-Nine

Hezekiah's Prayer for Healing (2 Kings 20; Isaiah 38)

King Hezekiah of Judah was known for his deep faith and commitment to God. During his reign, Hezekiah became seriously ill, and the prophet Isaiah came to deliver a message from God: **"Set your house in order, for you shall die; you shall not recover."** Faced with this grim prognosis, Hezekiah turned to God in prayer, seeking mercy and healing.

Hezekiah prayed earnestly, expressing his distress and pleading for God's intervention. In response to his sincere plea, God granted him an additional fifteen years of life and sent Isaiah back to deliver the good news. To commemorate this divine mercy, Hezekiah had the shadow cast on a sundial go back ten steps, symbolizing the extension of his life.

This incident not only saved Hezekiah's life but also strengthened his faith and reign. Hezekiah's heartfelt prayer exemplifies the power of turning to God in times of crisis, demonstrating that sincere prayer and trust in God's mercy can lead to miraculous outcomes.

Hezekiah's story underscores the importance of humility, repentance, and the power of prayer. It serves as an inspiring example of how faith can bring about God's grace and restoration even in the face of mortality.

Reflection for Today

1. Have you ever faced a life-threatening situation or a moment of intense fear? How did you seek God's help during that time?

2. What can you learn from Hezekiah's example about the importance of prayer and humility in seeking God's mercy?

Short Prayer

Merciful God, thank You for Hezekiah's example of earnest prayer and unwavering faith. Help me to turn to You in times of fear and uncertainty, seeking Your mercy and healing. Grant me the humility to recognize my need for Your grace and the strength to trust in Your promises. Amen.

Chapter Thirty

Esther Saves Her People (Book of Esther)

In the Persian Empire, under the reign of King Ahasuerus, a young Jewish woman named Esther found herself in a position of great influence. Esther, known for her beauty and grace, had been chosen as queen after a long search for a new wife for the king. However, Esther kept her Jewish identity a secret, as advised by her cousin and guardian, Mordecai.

Trouble arose when Haman, the king's high-ranking official, developed a deep-seated hatred for Mordecai, who refused to bow down to him. Consumed by his anger, Haman devised a sinister plan to exterminate all the Jews in the empire. He convinced King Ahasuerus to issue a decree that allowed for the annihilation of the Jewish people on a specific date.

When Mordecai learned of the decree, he was devastated and sought Esther's help. Despite the great risk involved—approaching the king without being summoned could result in death—Esther bravely decided to act. She fasted and prayed for three days, seeking God's guidance and strength.

With courage and determination, Esther approached the king and invited him and Haman to a series of banquets. During the second banquet, Esther revealed her Jewish identity and exposed Haman's plot to destroy her people. King Ahasuerus was enraged by Haman's deceit and ordered his immediate execution. Furthermore, the king issued a new decree allowing the Jews to defend themselves, leading to their salvation and the downfall of their enemies.

Esther's bravery and faith not only saved her people from destruction but also established the festival of Purim, a celebration of their deliverance. Her story is a powerful example of how one person's courage and trust in God can make a significant difference in the face of overwhelming odds.

Reflection for Today
- Have you ever had to stand up for what is right, even when it was difficult or risky? What did you learn from that experience?

- How can Esther's courage inspire you to take action in situations where others might remain silent?

- In what ways can you use your unique position or talents to help others and honor God?

Prayer
Dear Lord, help me to trust in Your plan and to have the bravery

to stand up for what is right, even when it's challenging. Grant me the wisdom to recognize opportunities to serve others and the strength to act with integrity and faith. May my actions bring glory to Your name and make a positive impact in the lives of those around me. Amen.

Chapter Thirty-One
Job's Trials (Book of Job)

Job was a wealthy and righteous man who was blessed with a large family, abundant livestock, and great honor in his community. However, Satan challenged Job's integrity, suggesting that Job was faithful only because of his prosperity. God allowed Satan to test Job by taking away his wealth, his children, and his health.

Despite immense suffering and the loss of everything he held dear, Job did not curse God. Instead, he maintained his faith, expressing profound sorrow but refusing to abandon his belief in God's goodness. Throughout his trials, Job grappled with understanding the reasons behind his suffering, engaging in deep conversations with his friends who tried to explain his misfortunes as a result of his own sins.

In the end, God responded to Job, not by providing direct answers, but by revealing the vastness of His creation and the limits of human understanding. Job acknowledged his limited perspective and repented for questioning God's wisdom. God restored Job's fortunes, granting him even greater blessings than before, including a new family and extended life.

Job's story highlights the complexities of faith in the face of inexplicable suffering. It teaches that trust in God does not always come with understanding but with a steadfast commitment to His goodness and sovereignty.

Reflection for Today

1. Have you ever faced inexplicable suffering or loss? How did you maintain your faith during those times?

2. What can Job's perseverance and trust in God teach you about handling adversity?

Prayer

Compassionate God, thank You for Job's unwavering faith amidst profound suffering. Help me to trust in Your goodness, even when I do not understand my circumstances. Grant me the strength to persevere and the humility to seek Your wisdom in all things. Amen.

Chapter Thirty-Two

JONAH AND THE BIG FISH (BOOK OF JONAH)

Jonah was a prophet called by God to deliver an important message to the people of Nineveh, a city known for its wickedness. Instead of obeying, Jonah decided to flee in the opposite direction, boarding a ship headed for Tarshish. As the ship sailed across the sea, a fierce storm arose, threatening to sink the vessel. The sailors, terrified, cast lots to find out who was responsible for the storm, and the lot fell on Jonah.

Realizing that he was the cause of their plight, Jonah admitted that he was running from God. He urged the sailors to throw him overboard to calm the storm. Reluctantly, they did so, and immediately the sea became calm. But Jonah's journey was far from over. God sent a great fish to swallow him, and Jonah spent three days and three nights in its belly.

Inside the dark and cramped space, Jonah prayed to God, expressing his repentance and gratitude for being saved from drowning. He acknowledged God's mercy and pledged to fulfill his mission. God heard Jonah's prayer and commanded the fish to vomit him onto dry land.

Determined to obey, Jonah traveled to Nineveh and delivered God's message: the city would be overthrown in forty days unless its people repented. To Jonah's surprise, the people of Nineveh believed God's warning. They fasted, wore sackcloth, and turned away from their evil ways. Even the king proclaimed a city-wide repentance. Seeing their genuine change of heart, God spared Nineveh from destruction.

Jonah, however, was displeased with God's mercy towards the Ninevites. He went outside the city and sulked, hoping to see its downfall. God used a plant to teach Jonah a lesson about compassion and mercy, showing him that just as he cared about the plant, God cared even more about the people of Nineveh.

Through this journey, Jonah learned about God's boundless mercy and the importance of obedience, even when it's difficult or contrary to our own desires.

Reflection for Today

- Have you ever tried to avoid a responsibility or task that you found challenging? What was the outcome?

- How does Jonah's story teach us about God's mercy and forgiveness?

- In what ways can you show compassion and understanding to others, even those who seem undeserving?

Prayer

Lord, please help me to trust in Your plans, even when they are difficult to follow. Grant me a compassionate heart to show kindness to others and the courage to fulfill the responsibilities You place before me. Amen.

Chapter Thirty-Three

Death & Resurrection of Jesus

As Jesus' ministry reached its climax, He faced increasing opposition from religious leaders who felt threatened by His teachings and growing influence. Knowing that His time on earth was coming to an end, Jesus made the ultimate sacrifice for humanity's salvation.

On the night before His crucifixion, Jesus gathered with His twelve disciples to celebrate the Passover meal, known as the Last Supper. During this intimate gathering, Jesus shared bread and wine, symbolizing His body and blood, establishing the new covenant between God and humanity. He instructed His disciples to remember Him through this act, even as He revealed that one of them would betray Him. Despite Jesus' love and trust, Judas Iscariot, one of the disciples, chose to betray Him for thirty pieces of silver. After the meal, Jesus went to the Garden of Gethsemane to pray, expressing His deep anguish about the suffering He was about to endure. He asked His Father to take the burden from Him, yet ultimately submitted to God's will, demonstrating His unwavering obedience and trust.

As Jesus prayed, Judas arrived with a crowd armed with swords and clubs, sent by the chief priests and elders. They seized Jesus, leading to His trial before the Sanhedrin, the Jewish ruling council, where false accusations were made against Him. Despite witnessing countless miracles and hearing His teachings, the council condemned Him for blasphemy. Jesus was brought before Pontius Pilate, the Roman governor, who found no fault in Him. However, fearing unrest and influenced by the crowd, Pilate succumbed to their demands and sentenced Jesus to be crucified. Mocked, beaten, and humiliated, Jesus carried His cross to Golgotha, where He was nailed to it between two criminals. As He suffered, He forgave those who persecuted Him and entrusted His spirit to God.

After several hours on the cross, Jesus breathed His last, signifying the completion of His sacrificial mission to atone for humanity's sins. A wealthy follower named Joseph of Arimathea requested Jesus' body and placed it in a tomb, sealing it with a large stone to honor Him. Three days later, women who were close to Jesus went to the tomb early in the morning, only to find the stone rolled away and the tomb empty. An angel announced that Jesus had risen from the dead, just as He had foretold. Over the next forty days, Jesus appeared to His disciples and many others, providing undeniable proof of His resurrection and reaffirming His teachings. Before ascending to heaven, Jesus promised to send the Holy Spirit to guide and empower His followers. His resurrection conquered death and offered eternal life to all who believe, fulfilling God's promise of redemption and hope.

The death and resurrection of Jesus are the cornerstone of Christian faith, demonstrating God's immense love and the promise of eternal life. Jesus' sacrifice provides a path for reconciliation with God, and His victory over death offers hope and assurance to believers worldwide.

Reflection for Today
- How does understanding Jesus' sacrifice influence your perspective on life and challenges?

- In what ways can you live out the hope and new life that Jesus' resurrection offers?

- How can the promise of the Holy Spirit empower you in your daily walk of faith?

Prayer

Heavenly Father, please Help me to live with the understanding of Your immense love and the promise of eternal life. Empower me with the Holy Spirit to face daily challenges with faith and to share Your love with others. Strengthen my belief in Your promises and guide me to live a life that honors You. Amen.

Chapter Thirty-Four

Daniel in the Lions' Den (Daniel 6)

Daniel was a highly respected official in the Persian Empire, serving under King Darius. His unwavering faith and integrity set him apart, making him a favorite in the king's court. However, Daniel's rise to prominence caused jealousy among other officials, who sought to bring him down. Unable to find any corruption in his work, they resorted to targeting his personal life—specifically, his steadfast commitment to his faith.

Knowing that Daniel prayed to God three times daily, the conspirators tricked King Darius into signing an edict that anyone who prayed to any god or human other than the king for thirty days would be thrown into the lions' den. Despite the threat, Daniel continued his daily prayers, showing his unwavering devotion to God.

When Daniel was caught praying, King Darius was filled with regret, but the law could not be broken. Reluctantly, he ordered

Daniel to be thrown into the den of lions. That night, the king could not sleep, consumed by worry for his faithful servant. Early the next morning, King Darius rushed to the lions' den and called out to Daniel, hoping against hope that he had been spared.

To everyone's astonishment, Daniel emerged unharmed. God had sent an angel to shut the lions' mouths, protecting him from harm. Overjoyed, King Darius ordered that those who had falsely accused Daniel be thrown into the lions' den instead. The lions immediately overpowered them, and King Darius issued a new decree praising Daniel's God, proclaiming His power and authority throughout the kingdom.

Daniel's miraculous deliverance from the lions' den was a powerful testament to God's sovereignty and faithfulness. It reinforced the importance of steadfast faith, even in the face of life-threatening opposition. Daniel's story inspired many, demonstrating that true faithfulness is rewarded and that God protects and honors those who serve Him faithfully.

Reflection for Today

1. Have you ever faced a situation where standing up for your beliefs was difficult or risky? How did you handle it?

2. How can Daniel's unwavering faith encourage you to remain steadfast in your own walk with God, even when faced with challenges?

Prayer

Faithful God, thank You for Daniel's example of unwavering faith in the face of danger. Help me to stand firm in my beliefs and trust in Your protection, even when circumstances are challenging. Strengthen my resolve to honor You in all situations. Amen.

Chapter Thirty-Five

BIRTH OF JESUS (MATTHEW 1–2; LUKE 2)

In a humble town called Bethlehem, the long-awaited Messiah was about to be born. Mary, a young woman engaged to Joseph, found out she was going to have a child by the Holy Spirit. Despite the uncertainty and potential scandal, Joseph chose to trust God and stood by Mary's side.

As the time approached for Mary to give birth, a decree from Caesar Augustus required everyone to return to their ancestral towns for a census. Mary and Joseph traveled from Nazareth to Bethlehem, Joseph's hometown, fulfilling the prophecy that the Messiah would be born there. However, the town was crowded, and there was no room available in the inns. With limited options, Mary gave birth to Jesus in a simple stable, laying Him in a manger because there was no place for them otherwise.

That night, shepherds in the nearby fields were visited by an angel who brought them joyous news: the Savior had been born. Suddenly, a multitude of heavenly hosts appeared, praising God and declaring peace on earth. The shepherds hurried to Bethlehem and found Mary, Joseph, and the newborn Jesus lying in the manger. They spread the word about what they had seen and heard, and all who heard it were amazed.

Meanwhile, wise men from the East, guided by a bright star, journeyed to honor the newborn King. They brought gifts of gold, frankincense, and myrrh, recognizing Jesus as the promised Savior. King Herod, feeling threatened by the news of a new king, sought to find and eliminate Him. However, God warned Joseph in a dream, and he took Mary and Jesus to Egypt to keep them safe. After Herod's death, they returned to Nazareth, where Jesus grew up surrounded by love and protection.

The birth of Jesus was a momentous event that brought hope and salvation to the world. Born in modest circumstances, Jesus' arrival fulfilled ancient prophecies and marked the beginning of a new chapter in God's plan for humanity.

Reflection for Today

- How does the humble birth of Jesus inspire you in your own life?

- In what ways can you share the good news of Jesus with those around you?

- How can you demonstrate trust in God during uncertain or challenging times?

Prayer

Heavenly Father, thank You for the incredible gift of Jesus and the hope His birth brings to the world. Help me to embrace humility and trust in Your plans for my life. Guide me to share Your love and the good news of Jesus with others, and strengthen my faith during times of uncertainty. May my actions reflect Your grace and bring glory to Your name. Amen.

Chapter Thirty-Six

Feeding the 5,000 (Mark 6; John 6)

Jesus and His disciples were traveling through a remote area, teaching and healing the people who came to hear Him. As the day went on, the crowd grew larger and larger, numbering about five thousand men, not including women and children. The disciples were concerned about how they would feed such a massive crowd, especially since they were in a desolate place with no immediate way to procure food.

Seeing the people's hunger, Jesus felt compassion for them. He asked His disciples, "Where shall we buy bread for these people to eat?" The disciples were perplexed, knowing there was no nearby town where they could gather provisions. Jesus then instructed them to feed the crowd themselves. They responded that they only had five loaves of bread and two fish—a meager offering for such a large group.

Undeterred, Jesus took the five loaves and two fish, looked up to heaven, and gave thanks. He then broke the loaves and distributed them to the disciples, who in turn handed them out to the people. Miraculously, everyone ate and was satisfied, and the disciples even collected twelve baskets full of leftover pieces. This incredible miracle demonstrated Jesus' divine power to provide abundantly, even from the smallest resources.

The feeding of the 5,000 is a powerful reminder of God's ability to supply our needs in unexpected ways. It highlights the importance of faith and obedience, showing that when we trust God and use what we have, He can accomplish great things beyond our imagination. This event also foreshadows the Last Supper and the ultimate provision of Jesus' body and blood for humanity's salvation.

Reflection for Today

- Have you ever faced a situation where resources seemed insufficient? How did you see God provide?

- In what ways can you use the gifts and talents God has given you to help others?

- How does this story encourage you to trust God with your needs and the needs of those around you?

Prayer

Lord Jesus, thank You for the miracle of the feeding of the 5,000 and for showing us Your limitless ability to provide. Help me to trust in Your provision, especially in times when resources seem scarce. Teach me to use the gifts and blessings You've given me to serve others and glorify Your name. Strengthen my faith to believe that with You, all things are possible. Amen.

Chapter Thirty-Seven
Sermon on the Mount (Matthew 5–7)

Early in His ministry, Jesus traveled to a hillside near the Sea of Galilee to teach a large crowd of His disciples and many others who had come to hear Him speak. This teaching session, known as the Sermon on the Mount, is one of the most profound and influential discourses recorded in the Bible.

As the sun rose, Jesus began by delivering the Beatitudes, a series of blessings that highlighted the values of God's kingdom. He spoke of the poor in spirit, those who mourn, the meek, those who hunger and thirst for righteousness, the merciful, the pure in heart, the peacemakers, and those who are persecuted for righteousness' sake. Each blessing revealed a deep spiritual truth, emphasizing humility, compassion, and a longing for God's will.

Jesus continued by teaching about the fulfillment of the law, explaining that He came not to abolish the commandments but to fulfill them. He challenged His listeners to move beyond mere outward obedience to embrace the spirit of the law, addressing issues like anger, lust, divorce, oaths, retaliation, and love for enemies. His teachings called for a transformation of the heart, urging His followers to pursue righteousness that surpasses that of the Pharisees.

One of the most well-known sections of the Sermon on the Mount is the Lord's Prayer. Jesus provided a model for prayer that focuses on honoring God's name, seeking His kingdom, requesting daily provision, forgiveness, and protection from temptation and evil. This prayer emphasizes dependence on God and the importance of aligning one's will with His.

Jesus also taught about the importance of sincerity in religious practices such as giving to the needy, praying, and fasting. He warned against performing these acts for public recognition, encouraging instead a private devotion that is pleasing to God alone. He used vivid illustrations, like storing up treasures in heaven rather than on earth, and taught the significance of the heart's intentions.

The sermon culminated in the well-known metaphor of the wise and foolish builders. Jesus compared those who hear His words and put them into practice to a wise man who built his house on a rock, able to withstand storms. In contrast, those who ignore His teachings are like a foolish man who built his house on sand, which collapses when faced with adversity.

Throughout the Sermon on the Mount, Jesus presented a radical vision of life under God's rule. His teachings called for integrity, mercy, purity, and a deep, genuine relationship with God and others. This sermon remains a foundational guide for Christian living, challenging believers to live out their faith with authenticity and love.

Reflection for Today

- Which part of the Sermon on the Mount resonates most with you, and why?

- How can you apply Jesus' teachings on sincerity and integrity in your daily life?

- In what ways can you build your "house" on the solid foundation of Jesus' words?

Prayer

Lord Jesus, please help me to understand and embrace the values of Your kingdom, living with humility, compassion, and integrity. Guide me to seek Your will in all that I do and to build my life on the solid foundation of Your Word. Empower me to live out my faith authentically and to reflect Your love in my interactions with others. Amen.

Chapter Thirty-Eight

Jesus' Baptism & Temptation (Matthew 3-4)

After His birth, Jesus grew up in Nazareth, living a life of quiet obedience and preparation. When He was about thirty years old, He began His public ministry, marking the start of a transformative journey that would change the world.

Jesus came to the Jordan River to be baptized by John the Baptist, a prophet calling people to repentance and preparation for the coming Messiah. John initially hesitated, feeling unworthy to baptize Jesus, but Jesus insisted, saying, "Let it be so now; it is proper for us to do this to fulfill all righteousness." As Jesus was baptized, the heavens opened, and the Spirit of God descended like a dove, resting on Him. A voice from heaven declared, "This is my beloved Son, with whom I am well pleased," affirming Jesus' divine identity and mission.

Immediately after His baptism, the Holy Spirit led Jesus into the wilderness, where He faced a period of intense testing. For forty days and nights, Jesus fasted and prayed, drawing strength from His Father. During this time, Satan approached Him, seeking to divert Him from His divine purpose. He tempted Jesus with three specific challenges:

1. **Turning Stones into Bread:** Recognizing Jesus' physical hunger, Satan urged Him to use His divine power to satisfy His needs. Jesus responded by quoting Scripture, emphasizing that "Man shall not live by bread alone, but by every word that comes from the mouth of God."

2. **Throwing Himself from the Temple:** Satan then took Jesus to the pinnacle of the temple, tempting Him to leap and prove His divine protection by having angels save Him. Jesus countered again with Scripture, stating, "You shall not put the Lord your God to the test."

3. **Offering All the Kingdoms of the World:** Finally, Satan offered Jesus all the kingdoms of the world in exchange for worship. Jesus firmly rejected this temptation, declaring, "Away from me, Satan! For it is written: 'Worship the Lord your God, and serve him only.'"

Each time, Jesus relied on God's Word to overcome temptation, demonstrating unwavering faith and obedience. After the forty days, angels came and attended to Him, preparing Him for the ministry ahead.

Jesus' baptism and subsequent temptation highlight His identification with humanity, His dependence on God, and His resistance to worldly temptations. This pivotal moment set the foundation for His teachings, miracles, and the ultimate sacrifice He would make for humanity's salvation.

Reflection for Today

- What temptations do you face in your daily life, and how can you rely on God's Word to overcome them?

- How does Jesus' example of obedience and reliance on God inspire you in your own walk of faith?

- In what ways can you prepare yourself spiritually for the challenges you encounter?

Prayer

Lord Jesus, thank You for Your example of unwavering faith and obedience. Help me to rely on Your Word when I face temptations and challenges. Strengthen my spirit and guide my actions so that I may follow Your path with integrity and trust in Your plan. Empower me to resist the things that lead me away from You and to grow closer to You each day. Amen.

Chapter Thirty-Nine

THE PRODIGAL SON (LUKE 15:11–32)

In a quiet village, there lived a wealthy man with two sons. The younger son, feeling restless and eager to explore life beyond his father's estate, approached him with a bold request for his share of the inheritance. Although it was unusual to divide an inheritance while the father was still alive, the father agreed, granting his son the financial freedom he sought.

With his newfound wealth, the younger son left home and embarked on a journey of indulgence and excess. He traveled to a distant country where he squandered his inheritance on lavish parties, extravagant living, and fleeting pleasures. For a time, he enjoyed the high life, but soon, his wealth dwindled, and a severe famine struck the land. Struggling to survive, the young man found himself destitute and desperate.

In his lowest moment, he took a job feeding pigs, a humiliating position for a Jewish man, and longed to eat the pods the pigs were eating. Realizing the depth of his mistakes, he reflected on his father's servants who had plenty to eat while he was starving. Filled with remorse, he decided to return home, hoping to work as one of his father's hired servants.

As he approached his father's house, rehearsing his apology, his father saw him from a distance and was filled with compassion. Running to his son, he embraced him tightly, ignoring any shame or resentment. The father ordered the best robe to be placed on him, a ring on his finger, and sandals on his feet. He also commanded the servants to prepare a celebratory feast, declaring, "For this son of mine was dead and is alive again; he was lost and is found."

Meanwhile, the older son, who had remained faithful and hardworking on the family estate, became angry upon hearing the celebration. He felt unappreciated and questioned his father's decision to lavishly welcome back his wayward brother. The father gently reminded him that everything he had belonged to the older son as well, but it was right to celebrate the return of someone who was lost and now found.

The story of the Prodigal Son beautifully illustrates themes of repentance, forgiveness, and unconditional love. It highlights the boundless mercy of the father, representing God, who eagerly welcomes back those who turn to Him, no matter how far they have strayed. It also challenges listeners to examine their own hearts, fostering a spirit of forgiveness and understanding towards others.

Reflection for Today

- Have you ever made a decision that led you away from what was right? How did you find your way back?

- How can you show forgiveness and understanding to someone who has wronged you?

- In what ways can you extend unconditional love and support to those who are struggling or have made mistakes?

Prayer

Heavenly Father, thank you for Your boundless mercy and forgiveness. Help me to recognize when I've strayed from Your path and give me the courage to return to You. Teach me to forgive others as You have forgiven me and to show unconditional love and compassion to those around me. Amen.

Chapter Forty

The Holy Spirit at Pentecost (Acts 2)

After Jesus ascended to heaven, His disciples returned to Jerusalem, as He had instructed them. They gathered together in an upper room, united in prayer and anticipation of what was to come. Pentecost, a Jewish festival celebrated fifty days after Passover, was approaching—a time when pilgrims from all over the region would descend upon Jerusalem.

As the disciples waited, suddenly a sound like a mighty rushing wind filled the entire house where they were sitting. They saw what seemed to be tongues of fire that separated and came to rest on each of them. Filled with awe and fear, they began to speak in other languages as the Spirit enabled them. People from various nations who were in

Jerusalem for Pentecost heard their voices and were amazed that each one was speaking in their native tongue.

Peter, one of the disciples, stood up and addressed the crowd. He explained that what they were witnessing was the fulfillment of the prophecy spoken by the prophet Joel: God would pour out His Spirit on all people. Peter boldly proclaimed that Jesus of Nazareth, who had been crucified and resurrected, was Lord and Messiah. He called the listeners to repent, be baptized in the name of Jesus Christ for the forgiveness of their sins, and receive the gift of the Holy Spirit.

That day, about three thousand people accepted Peter's message and were baptized. The believers devoted themselves to the apostles' teaching, fellowship, breaking of bread, and prayer. They shared their possessions, supported one another, and experienced unity and joy like never before. The Holy Spirit empowered them to spread the Gospel with boldness, leading to the rapid growth of the early Church.

The event of Pentecost marks the birth of the Christian Church, demonstrating the power and presence of the Holy Spirit in the lives of believers. It signifies the beginning of a new era where the Spirit guides, empowers, and unites followers of Christ, enabling them to live out their faith and share the Good News with the world.

Reflection for Today

- How do you experience the presence of the Holy Spirit in your daily life?

- In what ways can you rely on the Holy Spirit to empower you to share your faith with others?

- How can you foster a sense of community and unity like the early believers do today?

Prayer

Holy Spirit, thank You for coming to live within us and empowering us to live out our faith boldly. Help me to recognize Your presence in my daily life and to rely on Your guidance and strength. Teach me to share the love of Jesus with others and to build a community of believers that reflects Your unity and compassion. Fill me with Your wisdom and courage, and lead me to be a light in the world. Amen.

Chapter Forty-One
New Heaven and New Earth (Revelation 21–22)

After countless trials and tribulations, the Bible reveals a breathtaking vision of the future in the Book of Revelation. In chapters 21 and 22, the Apostle John describes the promise of a new creation, where God renews all things and dwells with His people in perfect harmony.

In this vision, John sees a new heaven and a new earth, for the first heaven and the first earth had passed away. The sea was no more, symbolizing the end of chaos and evil. John beholds the Holy City, the New Jerusalem, coming down out of heaven from God. The city shines with the glory of God, radiating light without the need for the sun or moon because God's presence illuminates it.

The gates of the New Jerusalem are made of precious jewels, and its foundations are adorned with every kind of gemstone. The streets are pure gold, clear as transparent glass, reflecting the magnificence of the city. A river of the water of life flows from the throne of God, and the tree of life stands on either side of the river, bearing twelve kinds of fruit and providing healing for the nations.

There is no more death, mourning, crying, or pain in this new creation. God Himself will wipe away every tear from their eyes. He will dwell with His people, and they will be His people. God will be with them, and He will be their God. They will reign forever and ever, experiencing eternal peace and joy in His presence.

This new creation is a place of ultimate restoration and fulfillment of God's promises. It represents the culmination of God's redemptive plan, where believers will live in eternal fellowship with Him, free from sin and suffering. The vision of the new heaven and new earth offers profound hope and assurance, reminding believers that God is faithful to bring about His perfect will.

Reflection for Today

- How does the promise of a new heaven and new earth influence your perspective on current challenges and suffering?

- In what ways can you live with hope and anticipation of God's ultimate restoration in your daily life?

- How can the vision of eternal fellowship with God shape your priorities and decisions today?

Prayer

Heavenly Father, thank You for the incredible promise of a new heaven and a new earth. Help me to hold onto this hope as I navigate the challenges of life. Strengthen my faith and encourage me to live in a way that reflects the eternal fellowship I have with You. May the vision of Your perfect creation inspire me to seek Your will and to trust in Your faithful plan for the future. Grant me peace and assurance as I look forward to the day when I will dwell with You forever. Amen.

Made in the USA
Monee, IL
30 March 2025